HAPPY MAGNET

By
Lemuel Abraham R

HAPPY MAGNET

This story is about a very special morning with my dad.

It was early, the sky still painted in soft shades of pink and orange as the sun began to rise.

We were driving back home from my athletics coaching.

Usually, I love these mornings, but that day, I felt a bit sad.

Dad noticed, of course. He always did.

What's troubling you, Lemuel? He asked gently.

His eyes flickering with concern as he glanced at me from the driver's seat.

I sighed, staring out the window at the fields rushing past. I don't know, Dad. I just feel...low.

Dad nodded thoughtfully, and for a few moments, we drove in silence.

Then he said, Lemuel, have you ever thought about magnets?

I turned to look at him, confused. Magnets?

Yes, Dad said, smiling. Magnets have a special power.

They can attract things to them. Imagine you are like a magnet.

A magnet?

I echoed, trying to understand where he was going with this.

Yes, a magnet, Dad continued. Magnets attract both Good & Bad things.

But you have a special power to choose what you attract.

If you decide to attract only good things, you can fill your life with happiness.

I thought about this and asked, But how do I make sure the magnet only attracts good things?

Dad smiled and explained, It's all about what you focus on, Lemuel.

If you think about happy things, like the fun you have during your athletics coaching, the friends you play with, and the things you love to do, your magic magnet will attract more of those good things.

But what if I still feel sad sometimes?

That's okay, Dad said kindly. Everyone feels sad sometimes.

When you do, try to find one small good thing to think about. Maybe it's remembering a funny joke, or thinking about your favorite toy.

Little by little, your magnet will start attracting more happiness.

As we drove home, I started thinking about all the good things I love.

I thought about running fast, playing with my friends and the yummy pancakes Dad makes for breakfast. I started to feel a little better.

You know what, Dad? I think my magnet is starting to work, I said with a smile.

Dad laughed and said, I think so too, Lemuel.

Just remember, you have the power to attract all the good things in the world.

From that day on, whenever I felt sad, I remembered Dads' story about the magic magnet.

And you know what? It really helped.

I learned that even on the toughest days, I could find something good to make me happy.

And that's the story of how I found my magic magnet. Thanks to my dad.

I hope you find your magic magnet too!